Jewish Theology

A Comparative Study

Barry L. Schwartz

BEHRMAN HOUSE, INC.

Dedicated to my wife, Debby,
and to my children, Nadav, Talia, and Noam.

COVER DESIGN: ROBERT J. O'DELL
PROJECT EDITOR: ADAM SIEGAL

11 EDISON PLACE, SPRINGFIELD, NEW JERSEY 07081
ISBN: 0-87441-523-3
MANUFACTURED IN THE UNITED STATES OF AMERICA

Contents

INTRODUCTION

To understand contemporary American Judaism, one must come to appreciate an exceedingly diverse theological spectrum. Among the major religious movements of American Judaism–Orthodox, Reform, Conservative and Reconstructionist–there are significant disparities in what we believe about God, Torah, and Israel. At the same time, however, there is a common affirmation of the importance of all three and the great wisdom to be found in the exploration of our 3,000-year tradition.

In examining the different movements, three questions immediately present themselves:

What are the basic similarities and differences between the branches of American Judaism?
What are the practical implications of their theological beliefs?
On what issues can we expect consensus or discord?

To answer these questions, I offer the reader a guided journey through primary sources. This compilation permits the thinkers and shapers of denominational Judaism to speak for themselves. In the best tradition of Jewish learning, this book requires the student to confront the text, to scrutinize with devotion the written word. Such study is often confined solely to ancient or medieval texts. As a result, important documents of contemporary Judaism are often neglected.

The collection of texts gathered here is presented in a comparative, thematic fashion, organized around four central issues: God, Torah, *halachah* (Jewish law), and Israel. Each of the subjects is viewed from the perspective of Judaism's four major movements: Orthodox, Reform, Conservative, and Reconstructionist. When possible, citations are taken from platform statements of a particular movement; presumably, this is as close to an official position or consensus opinion as exists. When such a text is unavailable, a prominent representative of a movement is selected. It should be emphasized that no source is likely to reflect a unanimity of opinion on a given issue. This is particularly true for those movements that permit or even encourage differences of belief and practice.

The rich tapestry of contemporary American Judaism is not confined, of course, to officially incorporated movements. As Mordecai Kaplan taught us, Jewish civilization extends far beyond the contribution of religious denominations. A brief selection of primary sources can not reveal the rich diversity within each movement. Yet the sources that follow do provide the student with a basic familiarity with the ideology of each major religious movement in American Judaism. Study of these sources is the first step in determining where you stand on that spectrum.

Orthodox Judaism

The Orthodox position is presented first. Orthodox is a term meaning "correct belief." In Judaism it has come to mean that segment of the Jewish community that is most traditional and adheres strictly to *halachah,* traditional Jewish law.

Modern Orthodoxy arose in nineteenth-century Germany. After the French Revolution, the doors of the ghetto (in Western Europe) were opened. Jews were finally given the same rights and privileges as the people among whom they lived. But with this new freedom, many Jews began questioning whether their traditional beliefs and practices would interfere with their ability to integrate into the society around them. Some Jews began to argue that sweeping changes in Jewish tradition needed to take place. Orthodox Judaism rejected this approach, maintaining a strict observance of traditional Jewish law.

Samson Raphael Hirsch (1808—1888), considered by many to be the spiritual father of modern Orthodox Judaism, sought to maintain adherence to *halachah* while still advocating the study of modern, secular disciplines. The Orthodox world to this day is divided between adherents of Hirsch's view and ultra-Orthodox groups that generally eschew secular learning and involvement. On the basic issues of theology, however, there is no major disagreement. All sides espouse a dogma that they view as consistent with that outlined by Maimonides and a succession of philosophers and *halachists*.

As a result of this *halachic* orientation, the Orthodox movement has not accepted many of the changes in ritual and liturgy embraced by the other movements. For example, Orthodox Judaism upholds the prohibition against ordaining women rabbis and cantors and permitting female Torah readers and leaders of prayer; separate seating for men and women in the synagogue is maintained. Prayers are recited only in Hebrew, and Sabbath observance prohibits automotive travel or activities that will require turning on electricity. *Kashrut* (dietary laws) and laws of personal status (concerning marriage, divorce, death, etc.), are upheld according to traditional *halachah*.

The modern Orthodox movement is organized around a congregational body known as the Union of Orthodox Jewish Congregations of America (UOJCA). Rabbis are trained primarily at the Theological Seminary of Yeshiva University in New York and become members of the Rabbinical Council of America (RCA). Yeshiva University also serves as the educational center for Orthodox leaders in many disciplines. The ultra-Orthodox community maintains its own organizational bodies and *yeshivot*. It is estimated that Orthodox Judaism accounts for 15 to 20 percent of America's affiliated Jewish community.

Reform Judaism

To maximize the contrasts often found on the theological spectrum, the Reform position is presented next. Also with roots in nineteenth-century Germany, Reform advocated evolution in Jewish ritual and thought in response to the changes brought about by the emancipation of Western European Jewry. With the new opportunities for citizenship and full participation in society, some Jews felt that certain traditional beliefs and practices were at best no longer relevant, at worst a hindrance to their attempt to lead a modern Jewish life.

Some reformers argued for radical change; others proposed more moderate action. The debate carried over to America's shores where Reform was organized into a national movement by Isaac Mayer Wise. The texts presented here are primarily representative of contemporary Reform, which more closely identifies with the proponents of moderation in ritual change. Nonetheless, in matters of broad doctrine, the texts reflect the Reform movement as a whole.

Reform has often led the way instituting change in Jewish prayer and ritual. From its inception, Reform argued for the equality of women in all religious matters, and the movement began ordaining women rabbis and cantors in the 1970s. By then the ceremony of bat mitzvah, as identical to bar mitzvah, had won widespread acceptance. Early on Reform introduced changes designed to enhance the esthetics of religious worship: prayer in the vernacular and musical accompaniment. Spurred by its identification with the prophetic heritage of the Bible, Reform advocated involvement in the general community's efforts to achieve social justice.

Not a few Reform decisions, however, remain bones of contention in the Jewish community. Among Reform's most controversial changes of late was the decision to accept patrilineal descent as a basis for determining whether a child is Jewish; previously, matrilineal descent was the only acceptable determinant. Reform's decision has led to the situation in which children born of a non-Jewish mother and Jewish father are considered Jewish by one segment of the Jewish community, the Reform community, but not by the others.

Reform congregations are members of the Union of American Hebrew Congregations (UAHC). Rabbis, cantors, educators, and communal service workers are trained at the Hebrew Union College–Jewish Institute of Religion (HUC–JIR), with campuses in New York, Cincinnati, Los Angeles, and Jerusalem. The Reform rabbinical organization is known as the Central Conference of American Rabbis (CCAR). Approximately 40 to 45 percent of the affiliated Jewish community identifies as Reform.

Conservative Judaism

The Conservative position is popularly characterized as occupying the middle ground between Orthodox and Reform. Its roots lie in dissatisfaction with early Reform coupled with a dissent from strict Orthodoxy. Some scholars link the beginning of the new movement with Zechariah Frankel's decision to walk out of a Reform rabbinical conference in Germany. The conference had decided that the use of the Hebrew language in much of the synagogue service was not necessary. Frankel considered this too great a break with tradition, and along with other rabbis dissatisfied with Reform, he founded a new school which would be more traditional in outlook, the Jewish Theological Seminary of Breslau. Others see the protest by some American rabbis over Reform's Pittsburgh Platform as the genesis of Conservative Judaism. As with Frankel, this protest led to the creation of a school, the Jewish Theological Seminary of New York. In America, the Conservative movement, under the direction of Solomon Schechter and others, flourished organizationally and ideologically.

The Conservative movement has attempted to articulate a unique school of thought which incorporates allegiance to *halachah* while at the same time admitting cautious change. The new unified Conservative platform, *Emet Ve-Emunah* (1988), reveals efforts to define consensus among diversity of opinion on even the most basic theological points.

Conservative Judaism's inherent caution and internal diversity have led to extensive debate on all proposed changes in ritual and law. Many of the decisions adopted by the majority have been resisted by a minority. In the mid-1980s the Conservative movement accepted the ordination of women rabbis. This followed acceptance of women as leaders of prayer, as Torah readers, and as participants in a minyan. Not all Conservative congregations accept these practices, however. After the ordination vote, a group of professors and rabbis broke from the mainstream Conservative movement to form their own, more traditional, organization. Some of these same individuals were opposed to a decision more than two decades earlier that permitted travel on the Sabbath for appropriate purposes.

The congregational arm of the Conservative movement is known as the United Synagogue of America (USA). Rabbis are trained at the Jewish Theological Seminary of America in New York (JTS), and become members of the Rabbinical Assembly (RA). Along with its West Coast affiliate, the University of Judaism, the Jewish Theological Seminary also trains cantors, educators, and communal service workers. Some 40 to 45 percent of the affiliated Jewish community are part of the Conservative movement.

Reconstructionist Judaism

The Reconstructionist movement, dwarfed in membership by the other branches, nevertheless occupies a distinct position on the Jewish spectrum. Its importance further transcends its size because of the influence it has exerted upon many individuals in Reform and Conservative Judaism. The only movement with exclusively American origins, Reconstructionism embodies the philosophy of one of this century's seminal Jewish thinkers, Mordecai Kaplan.

In essence, Kaplan proposed two new theses for what he termed the reconstruction of modern Judaism. The first might be called sociological, for it argued that Judaism should be viewed in much broader terms than doctrinal religion. Judaism needed to be evaluated in a new light, as the "civilization," or full cultural expression of a people. Religion was perhaps the most important component of Jewish civilization but by no means the exclusive one. Kaplan argued that our religious institutions should embody the whole of our civilization's heritage.

Kaplan's other thesis was theological, involving a bold new conception of God that drew inspiration from the insights of twentieth-century anthropology and philosophy. As will become apparent, Mordecai Kaplan strove to articulate a view of God in harmony with the rationalistic thinking characteristic of the modern era.

Given its cultural sensitivity and liberal theology, Reconstructionism has often led the way in introducing change in the Jewish world, despite its brief history. Many people are unaware, for example, that important innovations concerning the participation of women in the synagogue service actually began in the Reconstructionist movement, including the first bat mitzvah ceremony (of Kaplan's own daughter).

Reconstructionism, like Reform, is a strong advocate of ritual creativity and social involvement in the larger society. In fact, the Jewish Community Center as an institution owes a great deal to Kaplan's original conceptions in the 1920s and 1930s. In addition, the increase in educational and social programming by synagogues of all kinds was another response to the teachings of Kaplan.

Kaplan's Society for the Advancement of Judaism in New York (created in 1921) was the spiritual center of Reconstructionism for decades, but it was only in the 1960s that the movement achieved a distinct organizational identity. Today the Reconstructionists, like the other movements, have a congregational entity, called the Federation of Reconstructionist Congregations and Havurot (FRCH), a rabbinical seminary in Philadelphia known as the Reconstructionist Rabbinical College (RRC), and a rabbinical organization, the Reconstructionist Rabbinical Association (RRA). A very small percentage of the affiliated Jewish community is Reconstructionist.

Part I

GOD

What a movement believes about God will profoundly influence its entire ideological stance. Judaism has traditionally maintained that God is not only the creator of the world, but the revealer of law and wisdom, and the guiding hand of human affairs. What one believes about God will thus shape how one understands revelation (the sacred texts of Judaism) and history (including the mission and destiny of the people Israel).

Judaism has consistently professed a belief in one God, expressed by the central affirmation of Jewish worship, the Shema. Beyond this fundamental assumption, however, the texts that follow reveal widely varying views on such important issues as the extent of God's power, the ways in which God is involved with us, and the ways in which we are involved with God. What is more, it should become apparent that at least two of America's major religious movements deliberately refrain from articulating a specific dogma about God.

Theological debate and uncertainty notwithstanding, the quest for God through prayer, study, and deeds remains the primary spiritual concern of Judaism's religious movements. Above the ark in many synagogues throughout the country is the simple Hebrew sentence which proclaims: "Know Before Whom You Stand."

An Orthodox Perspective

Approaching the Text
The Nineteen Letters of Ben Uzziel

Samson Raphael Hirsch's statement reflects much of the traditional Jewish doctrine concerning God. The text underscores these characteristics of God's nature:

God is One
God is eternal
God is omnipotent (all-powerful)
God is omniscient (all-knowing)
God is beneficent (doing good)
God is transcendent (above nature)

Although Hirsch's statement deals primarily with God as Creator, traditional Jewish doctrine also speaks of God as Revealer (Giver of Torah) and Redeemer. This view maintains that God is continually active in the world, as opposed to the view (called deism) that God creates the world and then leaves it to run by natural law alone. Hirsch is adamant that all laws and forces are expressions of the Divine will. God is the source of whatever order we perceive, and the source of miracles that seemingly defy the natural order.

Two great questions arise from this conception of God. The first is the question of theodicy (*theo-*, God; *dicy*, justice: the problem of God's justice). If God is all-good and all-powerful, why is there evil in the world? Although there are various responses to this problem, the traditional response most often heard is that God's will is inscrutable. As the Book of Job asks: Who are we, mere mortals, to cast judgment on God's plan? For others, this kind of reply is insufficient. It is inconceivable that pain and suffering could be intentional on the part of the Divine. Individuals with such views often search out alternative conceptions of God. After the Holocaust, the question of theodicy is perhaps the greatest challenge to traditional Jewish conceptions of God.

The second great question arising from traditional theological speculation about God is one of providence. If God is all-powerful and all-knowing, do human beings have free will? Traditional Judaism responds with the idea that every individual is responsible for his or her own actions. Free will is the basis for our ability to pursue good or evil; however, our actions do not escape God's attention and each of us is ultimately rewarded or punished according to our deeds.

THE TEXT

Samson Raphael Hirsch (1808–1888) was the leading figure of German Orthodox Judaism in the nineteenth-century. Although strict in his obedience to halachah, *he advocated secular study in addition to Jewish education. Hirsch's considerable writings include his popular* The Nineteen Letters of Ben Uzziel, *from which this text is excerpted.*

"There is One God, one omnipotent Creator," the Torah proclaims, "Through His word all that is was created." Heaven and earth are His handiwork; His are the light and air, sea and dry land; His are the plants and fishes, birds, insects and all beasts; His the sun, moon and stars. He spoke–vayehi–and it was. Now behold separately each creation, from the blade of grass to the vast orb of the sun, each with its special purpose and each specially adapted in its form and matter for that purpose by the same Almighty wisdom. This Divine wisdom called to the light, "Serve the day"; to darkness, "Serve the night"; to the firmament, "Be the heaven over the earth"; to the gathering of waters, "Be the ocean"; to the dry substance, "Become thou the earth, the soil of life and development"; to the planets, "Be rulers of the seasons." Divine wisdom determined the purpose, and, in accordance with the purpose, ordained form, force and dimensions. He spoke–vayehi ken, and it was as it is, infinitesimally small or infinitely great. All was created by the Word of God, determined by His will, formed by His finger. To God, the Universal Force, belong all the forces which are at work in nature and the universe and all the laws which regulate life: from the force and the law which govern the fall of the stone or the growth of the seed, to those which determine the orbit of the planets or the unfolding of the human mind.

Probing the Text

1. What is God's relationship to nature as described in this passage?
2. What other possible God-nature relationships can you describe?
3. If God is omnipotent, as Hirsch claims, how would Hirsch respond to the question of why there is evil in the world?
4. Why do you suppose God would choose to grant free will to human beings?

A Reform Perspective

<u>Approaching the Text</u>
Columbus Platform
San Francisco Platform

To the extent that the rabbinic platforms represent the movement as a whole, Reform Judaism has consistently espoused the idea of belief in God as central to Judaism. In fact, the Columbus Platform (1937) reaffirms traditional notions of God as One, living (active), creating, lawgiving and redeeming. There is nothing in this brief statement that contradicts Orthodox Judaism! The differences are manifest in other categories examined in subsequent chapters of this book.

The tenor of the San Francisco Platform (1976), composed almost four decades after the Columbus Platform, is less self-assured in its declaration about God. The San Francisco Platform seeks to reaffirm belief in God as central, without specifying the content of that belief. It seeks to be as inclusive as possible, recognizing the widely varying God beliefs that typify the contemporary movement. The Platform recognizes that both recent history (especially the Holocaust) and "challenges to modern culture" have made it more difficult for some people to affirm God.

The texts as a whole might strike you as rather brief, vague, and incomplete. The Reform movement has not published a more comprehensive position. Even these words have been criticized for misrepresenting the supposed majority viewpoint of the movement. In the absence of survey data or published collective opinion, it is difficult to assess if a prevailing view about God exists at all. Individual essays abound, demonstrating that within Reform there can be found adherents of almost every theological orientation concerning God. On the basis of the platforms it can be concluded that Reform, while affirming belief in God, does not espouse a particular dogma about the nature of God.

THE TEXT

The three "Platforms of Reform Judaism" are the products of rabbinic gatherings of the movement in 1875 (Pittsburgh), 1937 (Columbus), and 1976 (San Francisco). While not official expressions of doctrine, they have been influential in determining the nature of Reform ideology and practice. The accompanying text is excerpted from the Columbus and San Francisco Platforms.

Columbus Platform 1937

The heart of Judaism and its chief contribution to religion is the doctrine of the One, living God, who rules the world through law and love. In Him all existence has its creative source and mankind its ideal of conduct. Through transcending time and space, He is the indwelling Presence of the world, we worship Him as the Lord of the universe and as our merciful Father.

San Francisco Platform 1976

The affirmation of God has always been essential to our people's will to survive. In our struggle through the centuries to preserve our faith we have experienced and conceived of God in many ways. The trials of our own time and the challenges to modern culture have made steady belief and clear understanding difficult for some. Nevertheless, we ground our lives, personally and continually, on God's reality and remain open to new experiences and conceptions of the Divine. Amid the mystery we call life, we affirm that human beings, created in God's image, share in God's eternality despite the mystery we call death.

PROBING THE TEXT

1. What do the authors mean by "the trials of our time and the challenges to modern culture"?

2. How have these "trials" and "challenges" affected some people's view of God?

3. What do the authors mean by the phrase "human beings ... share in God's eternality"?

4. In light of the San Francisco Platform, can a Reform Jew be an agnostic or an atheist?

A Conservative Perspective

Approaching the Text
Emet Ve-Emunah

Emet Ve-Emunah is a very recent document. Like the most recent Reform platform, it seeks to be as inclusive as possible. The text recognizes the significant diversity of opinion within the Conservative movement. In the same spirit as Reform, it begins by affirming the critical importance of belief in God but explicitly acknowledges that Conservative Judaism does not "specify all the particulars." The statement then goes on to present two alternative views of God.

The first conception of God is basically the traditional view. It is linked with those who understand the Bible as God's revealed word. Most of the paragraph is devoted not to a description of divine attributes, but to an exposition of the grounds for maintaining such belief. They include all the classic arguments for the existence of a supreme Creator and Lawgiver.

The second conception of God is linked with more recent philosophical thinking. This section seems to be an attempt to acknowledge a significant Reconstructionist influence within Conservative Judaism. It should be noted that Reconstructionism initially began as a school of thought within Conservative Judaism and only later became a distinct movement. The breaking point was not so much Reconstructionism's new ideas about God, but its refusal to accept the unconditional binding authority of traditional Jewish law. The clue in this text to the influence of Reconstructionist theology (to be examined in the next section of this book) is the sentence: "[God is] present when we look for meaning in the world, when we work for morality, for justice, and for future redemption."

The Conservative statement may also be alluding to the thought of another important twentieth-century philosopher, Martin Buber. One of Buber's primary ideas was that God cannot be proven or rationalized. God can only be encountered. For Buber, the real content of religion emerged out of experiencing a profound relationship with another person or with God. Buber called the mundane kind of relationship that often exists between people and objects (animate or inanimate) "I-It." However, when people transcended that relationship with each other and with God, treating the other not as an object but as worthy of full concern and care, then the result was what he termed "I-Thou." The clue in the text to Buber's influence are the words, "the existence of God is not a 'fact' that can be checked against the evidence. Rather, God's presence is the starting point."

It is evident that the Conservative movement is willing to accept a wide range of views concerning God. The influence of a theologically diverse group of thinkers, most notably Mordecai Kaplan, Martin Buber, and Abraham Joshua Heschel (a traditionalist influence), has only widened the spectrum of views over the years. As with Reform, no one conception of God can be said to speak for the movement as a whole.

The Text

This text is from Emet Ve-Emunah, *subtitled:* Statement of Principles of Conservative Judaism. *It is the unified statement of the movement, published in 1988. Joining in the platform were all three major bodies of the Conservative movement: the Jewish Theological Seminary, the Rabbinical Assembly, and United Synagogue of America.*

Conservative Judaism affirms the critical importance of belief in God, but does not specify all the particulars of that belief. Certainly, belief in a trinitarian God, or in a capricious, amoral God can never be consistent with Jewish tradition and history. Valid differences in perspective, however, do exist.

For many of us, belief in God means faith that a supreme, supernatural being exists and has the power to command and control the world through His will. Since God is not like objects that we can readily perceive, this view relies on indirect evidence. Grounds for belief in God are many. They include the testimony of Scripture, the fact that there is something rather than nothing, the vastness and orderliness of the universe, the sense of command that we feel in the face of moral imperatives, the experience of miraculous historical events, and the existence of phenomena which seem to go beyond physical matter, such as human consciousness and creativity. All of these perceptions are encounters that point beyond us. They reinforce one another to produce an experience of, and thus a belief in, a God who, though unperceivable, exists in the usual sense of the word. This is the conception of God that emerges from a straightforward reading of the Bible.

Some view the reality of God differently. For them, the existence of God is not a "fact" that can be checked against the evidence. Rather, God's presence is the starting point for our entire view of the world and our place in it. Where is such a God to be found and experienced? He is not a being to whom we can point. He is, instead, present when we look for meaning in the world, when we work for morality, for justice, and for future redemption. A description of God's nature is not the last line of a logical demonstration: It emerges out of our shared traditions and stories as a community. God is, in this view as well, a presence and a power that transcends us, but His nature is not completely independent of our beliefs and experiences. This is a conception of God that is closer to the God of many Jewish philosophers and mystics.

The two views broadly characterized here have deep roots in the Bible and in the rest of Jewish tradition. They are both well represented in Conservative Jewish thought.

Probing the Text

1. According to the text, what are the two primary conceptions of God?
2. What are the six arguments for the existence of God advanced here? Can you develop a line of reasoning supporting each one?
3. Can we pray and refer to God in personal terms if, as the second view suggests, "He is not a being to whom we can point"?
4. What is meant by the statement, "His nature is not completely independent of our beliefs and experiences"?

A Reconstructionist Perspective

Approaching the Text

The Meaning of God in Modern Jewish Religion

Mordecai Kaplan presents a conception of God that is radically different from that of traditional Judaism. Kaplan shies away from describing God in terms of a personal being, preferring instead the word "force" or "power." In this view God is not omnipotent and omniscient, but dependent, as it were, on our actions. God is present to the extent that we strive after our highest ideals. God remains the transcendent creative and moral force of the world. God is the source of human love, courage, morality, and creativity.

Kaplan's conception of God is often termed "religious naturalism" because it postulates a God that works through nature (trans-natural) and not above nature (super-natural). Although God is not the same as nature, God is manifest to us only through our experience of natural and moral law. In this sense, Reconstructionism does not accept ideas of revelation or miracles that contradict our understanding of the natural order.

The Reconstructionist view of God, as set forth by Kaplan, has been severely criticized by traditionalists on a number of grounds. First and foremost is the argument that any attempt to limit God's power and providence flies in the face of rabbinic teaching. According to traditional doctrine, God, as the creator of the universe, can act independent of the laws of nature at will. Any attempt to limit God's dominion, from an Orthodox perspective, would seem to suggest an alternative power to God's. So controversial was Kaplan's new theology that soon after his first works were published he was excommunicated by a group of Orthodox rabbis.

A second criticism of Kaplan's theology is the perception that his rationalism lacks warmth and spirituality. A frequently heard question is: How can one pray to an idea or a force? In the same vein: How can a view of God that is so conceptual and impersonal engender the kind of human—God relationship that inspires and commands? If God is not the One who can respond to individual petition, why pray?

The Text

Mordecai Kaplan (1881–1983), one of the twentieth-century's most influential Jewish philosophers, founded the Reconstructionist movement in the 1940s. His ideas are contained in more than a dozen books, among them: Judaism as a Civilization *(1934) and* The Meaning of God in Modern Jewish Religion *(1937), from which this text is excerpted.*

But it is an undeniable fact that there is something in the nature of life which expresses itself in human personality, which evokes ideals, which sends men on the quest of personal and social salvation. By identifying that aspect of reality with God, we are carrying out in modern times the implications of the conception that man is created in God's image. For such an identification implies that *there is something divine in human personality, in that it is the instrument through which the creative life of the world effects the evolution of the human race.* The corollary of the thought of man's likeness to God has always been the sense of the sacredness of human personality, of its inherent worth.

This should not be interpreted as implying that the belief in God is purely subjective, a figment of the imagination rather than an interpretation of reality. One might as well say that, since the awareness of color is a subjective experience, it is entirely a creation of the eye, and that no objective reality is responsible for the eye experiencing color, as to say that, since our idea of God is determined wholly by our own limited experience of life's values, there is no objective reality which is responsible for the values which we experience. *The word "God" has thus come to be symbolically expressive of the highest ideals for which men strive and, at the same time, points to the objective fact that the world is so constituted as to make for the realization of those ideals.*

PROBING THE TEXT

1. How would you define God from a Reconstructionist viewpoint?
2. What can God do, and not do according to such a view?
3. What is problematic about this conception of God?
4. In light of the Reconstructionist view of God, how would you describe the purpose of prayer?

Part II

TORAH

The idea of one God is shared by other religious traditions. So too is the general notion of Divine revelation. Unique to Judaism, however, is the concept of Torah.

Originally, Torah was taken to mean the written law (Tanach) alone. Rabbinic Judaism expanded the concept of Torah to include the so-called oral law (Talmud). Even though the Talmud was acknowledged to have been written by later sages, they were said to have acted under a prophetic inspiration that stemmed from the original revelation to Moses at Sinai. According to the Talmud, prophecy and the authority to establish new law ceased as the Talmud was being completed. In other words, the Sages put self-closure on the process of revelation by contending that they were the last generations to receive the dictates of Divine will. Although the movements of modern Judaism differ on what constitutes Torah, how it was created, and the extent of its authority, all agree that it is the foundation of Judaism.

It will become apparent in this chapter that the great debate among the movements of Judaism is whether the Torah is the directly revealed word of God or the indirectly revealed (humanly written, divinely inspired) word of God. Not to be overlooked, however, is the fact that Torah, however defined and understood, remains a kind of blueprint for the observance of Judaism. Some may adopt the blueprint as it was once drawn, others may modify specifications, but the basic plan remains in use.

An Orthodox Perspective

Approaching the Text
The Condition of Jewish Belief

There are essentially two basic views of revelation in Judaism: Orthodox and liberal. To a large extent, which school you subscribe to is determined by how you answer the question: Who wrote the Torah?

This text presents the Orthodox response. Norman Lamm is unequivocal in the belief that the Torah is God-given. God's revelation of the Torah took place at one time, in one place, to one people–Israel–standing at the foot of Mount Sinai. According to Lamm, one need not comprehend precisely how God communicates with Moses to hold this view. The process of revelation is not given to rational explanation. Nor does holding the view that the Torah is God-given mean that the Torah text is subject to only a literal interpretation. As Lamm points out, language is an imperfect instrument, though still the best means of collective communication. All written language must be interpreted by the reader. The crucial point is that whatever the interpretation, the text is still viewed as an explicit expression of God's will.

Orthodox Torah commentary does not employ the critical/scientific approach that is common to modern scholarship. The reason is not hard to understand. Most modern biblical scholarship rests on the assumption of human authorship of the Torah and suggests that the Torah is a collection of many different sources and documents edited together. It suggests that these texts have changed over time. Orthodox Judaism, on the other hand, holds that the Torah is immutable, unchanging and unchangeable for all time.

THE TEXT

Norman Lamm has long been a leading figure in the modern Orthodox community. He is president of Yeshiva University and has authored numerous books and articles. This text is taken from The Condition of Jewish Belief, *a symposium compiled by the editors of* Commentary *magazine in 1966.*

I believe the Torah is divine revelation in two ways: in that it is God-given and in that it is godly. By "God-given," I mean that He willed that man abide by His commandments and that that will was communicated in discrete words and letters. Man apprehends in many ways: by intuition, inspiration, experience, deduction–and by direct instruction. The divine will, if it is to be made known, is sufficiently important for it to be revealed in as direct, unequivocal, and unambiguous a manner as possible, so that it will be understood by the largest number of the people to whom this will is addressed. Language, though so faulty an instrument, is still the best means of communication to most human beings.

Hence, I accept unapologetically the idea of the verbal revelation of the Torah. I do not take seriously the caricature of this idea which reduces Moses to a secretary taking dictation. Any competing notion of revelation, such as the various "inspiration" theories, can similarly be made to sound absurd by anthropomorphic parallels. Exactly how this communication took place no one can say: it is no less mysterious than the nature of the One who spoke. The divine–human encounter is not a meeting of equals, and the *kerygma* that ensues from this event must therefore be articulated in human terms without reflecting on the mode and form of the divine *logos*. *How* God spoke is a mystery; how *Moses* received this message is an irrelevancy. *That* God spoke is of the utmost significance, and *what* He said must therefore be intelligible to humans in a human context, even if one insists upon an endlessly profound mystical overplus of meaning in the text. To deny that God can make His will clearly known is to impose upon him a limitation of dumbness that would insult the least of His human creatures.

Probing the Text

1. How does Norman Lamm understand the way in which the Torah was communicated to us?

2. According to Lamm, is the Torah perfect?

3. Why does Lamm accept varying interpretations of Torah if it is God's word?

4. What objections would a rationalist have with this view of revelation?

A Reform Perspective

<u>Approaching the Text</u>
The Growth of Reform Judaism

At the very outset of the text in this section, Julian Morgenstern defines the central theological difference between Orthodox and Reform Judaism: does one believe that the Torah was dictated by God or by humans? Morgenstern contends that any process of reform is predicated on viewing the Torah as a human document. Otherwise, in his opinion, there is no justification for making any change in God's revelation.

Morgenstern articulates a view of Torah that might be termed "indirect revelation," in contrast to Orthodoxy's doctrine of "direct revelation." Indirect revelation acknowledges the role of Divine inspiration in the composition of Torah. While the Torah may not be the direct word of God, it is nevertheless inspired by God.

The concept of Divine inspiration is referred to consistently in Reform Judaism but is often employed ambiguously. Just what does Divine inspiration mean? Just what parts of the Bible are inspired? Morgenstern does not associate inspiration with prophecy, which would be in keeping with traditional Jewish understanding. Rather, he understands Torah as the record of a people's encounter with God. It is Israel's diary, as it were: a people's thoughts about God, feelings about God, and attempts to be godlike. In this sense much of the Torah is a unique source of moral and spiritual instruction.

Like every human document, however, the written Torah is imperfect and subject to the inherent limitations of particular individuals writing at particular times. The Torah's commandments, therefore, should not be viewed as eternally authoritative edicts. Reform maintains that the Torah reflects one particular stage in Jewish evolution. Divine inspiration is not limited to the written or oral law. Reform argues that we continue to gain insight about God's intention in every generation so that Revelation should be understood as an ongoing process rather than a single event.

THE TEXT

Julian Morgenstern (1881–1976) was president of the Reform movement's rabbinical seminary, Hebrew Union College, for three decades. He was a noted biblical scholar who championed a modern critical approach to Scripture.

"Is the Torah, in the literal sense in which our fathers understood it, divinely revealed; that is, were its laws actually established by God and communicated, whether in writing or orally, by Him to Moses and through Moses to Israel?" If the answer be "Yes," then the only conclusion possible is that the laws of the Torah, one and all, are eternally and indissolubly binding upon all Israel. Only if the answer to the question be "No," only if, after careful, earnest, conservative and reverent research, we are forced to conclude that the laws of the Torah are of altogether human origin, and that only for certain, easily comprehended, historical reasons were they represented as having been given by God to Moses, are we justified in abrogating or altering even the least of these laws. Otherwise no reform is justifiable, even under the plea of historical necessity or "the spirit of the age." Either we hold the Torah to be, as our fathers believed, in the most literal sense of divine origin, and therefore all its laws eternally binding upon all Israel, and all reform in Judaism, which would entail disregard or abrogation of even a single one of these laws, out of the question; or else we must hold the firmly established and absolutely irrefutable conclusion that the Torah and the entire Bible are, in the literal sense at least, the result of human effort, human knowledge and human religious insight, inspiration and revelation. Logically reform in Judaism may only follow, and never precede, this conclusion.

Nor does Biblical Science deny, as so many of its opponents claim, the inspiration of the Bible. On the contrary, it feels therein a larger and fuller measure of inspiration than the traditionalist can ever conceive of. For it interprets the Bible as the record of Israel's thinking about God and feeling after Him and of the knowledge of Him which was revealed to it, and which it, therefore, discovered and came to possess, through a thousand or more years of its early history. In this light, not merely the laws, and not merely a certain few of the stories, and not merely the Torah, are inspired, but every book, every story, every chapter. For all bespeak something of Israel's search after God and record something of the knowledge of God which has been revealed to Israel. In this sense Israel was indeed God's chosen people, His inspired people, upon whom His spirit truly rested, whose entire history, therefore, was guided and inspired by Him. And certainly the record of this history, the only record preserved to us of all Israel's ancient literature, is truly inspired too. It is no mere ordinary, human record or book. It is in no sense like any other book. It is the inspired and inspiring record of God, working with His people and leading them on to an ever higher, fuller and truer knowledge of Himself.

PROBING THE TEXT

1. Why does Morgenstern believe that the Reform view of Torah "feels therein a larger and fuller measure of inspiration than the traditionalist can ever conceive of"?

2. According to the Reform view, is it possible to claim with certainty that any particular command of the Torah is God's will?

3. What authority does Torah have from a Reform perspective?

4. What do you think the early reformers meant by the term "progressive revelation"?

A Conservative Perspective

Approaching the Text
Emet Ve-Emunah

While Conservative Jews do not necessarily agree about the extent of human involvement in the giving of the Torah, they view it as more than Moses recording God's communication. For many, the Torah is a Divinely inspired but humanly written document. This premise is not unlike the inspiration-based beliefs of some more traditionally minded Reform thinkers. Admitting a human component in the content of revelation, as opposed to the belief in a completely Divine creation, is the divide that separates liberal from Orthodox Judaism.

Conservative Judaism understands revelation as a continuous process. While it terms Sinai the "greatest event," the statement stresses that revelation is ongoing. Orthodox Judaism, it will be remembered, limits the content of revelation to the Bible and Talmud. Conservative Judaism contends that God's communication "remains alive in the Codes and Responsa to the present day."

It should also be noted that the Conservative text's final paragraph introduces an idea that is essentially Reconstructionist in nature. Recall that in the Conservative statement about God we also identified an effort to include Reconstructionist thought within the ranks of acceptable Conservative doctrine. Here the key sentence is: "Others among us conceive of revelation as the continuing discovery, through nature and history, of truths about God and the world." As the next text will demonstrate, Reconstructionist Judaism understands revelation more as our discovery of wisdom and truth than as miraculous disclosures of Divine will through prophecy. This view of revelation presents Torah as one of many possible sources of Divine truth.

THE TEXT

This text is from Emet Ve-Emunah, *subtitled:* Statement of Principles of Conservative Judaism. *It is the unified statement of the movement, published in 1988. Joining in the platform were all three major bodies of the Conservative movement: the Jewish Theological Seminary, the Rabbinical Assembly, and United Synagogue of America.*

Conservative Judaism affirms its belief in revelation, the uncovering of an external source of truth emanating from God. This affirmation emphasizes that although truths are transmitted by humans, they are not a human invention. That is why we call the Torah *torat emet.* The Torah's truth is both theoretical and practical, that is, it teaches us about God and about our role in His world. As such, we reject relativism, which denies any objective source of authoritative truth. We also reject fundamentalism and literalism, which do not admit a human component in revelation, thus excluding an independent role for human experience and reason in the process.

The nature of revelation and its meaning for the Jewish people have been understood in various ways within the Conservative community. We believe that the classical sources of Judaism provide ample precedents for these views of revelation.

The single greatest event in the history of God's revelation took place at Sinai, but was not limited to it. God's communication continued in the teaching of the Prophets and the biblical Sages, and in the activity of the Rabbis of the Mishnah and the Talmud, embodied in Halakhah and the Aggadah (law and lore). The process of revelation did not end there; it remains alive in the Codes and Responsa to the present day.

Some of us conceive of revelation as the personal encounter between God and human beings. Among them there are those who believe that this personal encounter has propositional content, that God communicated with us in actual words. For them, revelation's content is immediately normative, as defined by rabbinic interpretation. The commandments of the Torah themselves issue directly from God. Others, however, believe that revelation consists of an ineffable human encounter with God. The experience of revelation inspires the verbal formulation by human beings of norms and ideas, thus continuing the historical influence of this revelational encounter.

Others among us conceive of revelation as the continuing discovery, through nature and history, of truths about God and the world. These truths, although always culturally conditioned, are nevertheless seen as God's ultimate purpose for creation. Proponents of this view tend to see revelation as an ongoing process rather than as a specific event.

Probing the Text

1. In what way does this statement differ from that of Orthodox Judaism?
2. In what way does it differ from that of Reform Judaism?
3. What are the possible consequences of so much diversity of opinion within the Conservative movement?
4. Do you think there is a uniquely Conservative conception of Torah?

A Reconstructionist Perspective

Approaching the Text

The Reconstructionist Prayer Book

Reconstructionist Judaism unequivocally identifies with the liberal view of the Torah as a humanly written document. In Kaplan's words: "The truth is not that God revealed the Torah to Israel, but that the Torah has...revealed God to Israel." In actuality, Reconstructionist Judaism could not have it any other way. Mordecai Kaplan's philosophy, which remains the guiding approach of the movement, denies that God acts in supernatural ways. Consequently, revelation can be no more, or less, than the discovery of religious truths through our own natural powers of perception. Kaplan explicitly calls this process of discovery revelation. Revelation is real because there are truths to be discovered and the human ability to accomplish the task.

Without the benefit of supernatural Divine communication, however, a series of questions arise that apply to all liberal Judaism and their views on revelation:

What really happened at Sinai?
Which parts of the Torah represent genuine religious truth, and which do not?
Who decides the above question?
Which commandments should be observed?
Why should the commandments be observed?

Like Reform, Reconstructionist Judaism emphasizes the continuing significance of Torah, even if its authority can no longer be considered absolute. As a repository of wisdom about Israel's search for God, it is unrivaled. The reading and study of Torah spur our own spiritual quest. In these historical and spiritual senses, the Torah is inspirational and sacred. Since the discovery of religious truth is never ending, we too add our part to Torah.

THE TEXT

Mordecai Kaplan (1881–1983), one of the twentieth-century's most influential Jewish philosophers, founded the Reconstructionist movement in the 1940s. His ideas are contained in more than a dozen books, among them Judaism as a Civilization *(1934) and* The Meaning of God in Modern Jewish Religion *(1937). This statement is excerpted from the introductory section of the* Reconstructionist Prayer Book *(1945), edited by Kaplan and a group of his early disciples.*

Tradition affirms that God supernaturally revealed the Torah in its present text, to Moses on Mount Sinai. But the critical analysis of the text by modern scholars and the scientific outlook on history render this belief no longer tenable. We now know that the Torah is a human document, recording the experience of our people in its quest for God during the formative period of its history. The sacredness of the Torah does not depend upon its having been supernaturally revealed. The truth is not that God revealed the Torah to Israel, but that the Torah has, in every successive generation, revealed God to Israel. It can still reveal God to us. Though we no longer assume that every word in the text is literally or even figuratively true, the reading of the Torah enables us to relive, in imagination, the experiences of our fathers in seeking to make life conform to the will of God, as they understood it. We thus make this purpose of theirs our own and are inspired to seek God also in our own experiences. And those who seek God find Him. Our discovery of religious truth is God's revelation to us.

The study of Torah in this spirit is properly the central act of worship. It is, moreover, indispensable to our survival and growth as a people. The Torah so conceived is indeed a "tree of life" everlasting, planted within us. But it cannot serve this purpose as long as the Synagogue bases the authority of the Torah on the dogma of supernatural revelation, which the modern mind rejects. We have, accordingly, deemed it necessary to stress the sacredness of the Torah in other ways than by affirming that it was supernaturally revealed to Moses on Mount Sinai.

PROBING THE TEXT

1. What does Kaplan mean when he writes, "The truth is not that God revealed the Torah to Israel, but that the Torah has, in every successive generation, revealed God to Israel"?
2. If the sacredness of the Torah does not depend upon its having been supernaturally revealed, what does make the Torah sacred?
3. Are there any differences between the Reform and Reconstructionist views of Torah?
4. What does Kaplan mean when he states, "Our discovery of religious truth is God's revelation to us"?

Part III

HALACHAH

Many Jews argue that allegiance to *halachah*, more than anything else, has sustained Judaism and the Jewish people. *Halachah* is the traditional Jewish law contained in the Torah and the Talmud. The word *halachah* actually comes from the Hebrew root meaning "to go" or "to walk." *Halachah* is the way, or path, that a Jew is commanded to follow.

Halachah was intended to govern all aspects of life; it is what we would consider today as civil and religious law. The body of regulations that comprise *halachah* deal with everything from agriculture and business to prayer and charity. In previous eras, rabbis and leaders of the Jewish community were charged with enforcing *halachah* throughout the community.

The question of *halachah*'s authority is naturally linked to one's view of Torah and is thus very much a subject of debate in the Jewish community. Two of Judaism's four major movements accept the binding nature of *halachah*, and two do not. But the questions concerning *halachah* are not limited to authority. They extend to who should determine what *halachah* says, and how. On these issues the movements disagree not only with each other, but within themselves!

When considering the issue of *halachah* from a comparative denominational perspective, three questions are crucial:

> Is *halachah* binding upon the Jewish people?
> Can *halachah* be changed if need be?
> Who should interpret *halachah*, and how?

This trio of questions on authority, change, and interpretation, are the issues most responsible for the denominational divisions in contemporary Judaism. Almost everyone would agree, however, that the accumulated wisdom of more than 2,000 years of *halachah* is the starting point for informed Jewish decision making.

An Orthodox Perspective

Approaching the Text

The Condition of Jewish Belief

Orthodox Judaism defines *halachah* to mean Jewish law derived from the Torah (Tanach, or Bible, and Talmud). Given the Orthodox view of revelation already examined, it should come as no surprise that Berkovits views *halachah* as eternally binding.

According to Orthodoxy, no change in *halachah* is permissible, as God's word is eternally valid. Human beings cannot presume to tamper with Divinely revealed law. Maimonides made clear that one is not allowed to add or subtract even a single command. At most, we can only interpret, or apply, *halachah*. Berkovits notes that Judaism presents a rich tradition of Torah interpretation. That is why some Orthodox thinkers argue that there is no Jewish fundamentalism. Even the Talmudic Sages recognized meanings in the text beyond the literal, although the law itself, however understood, remains immutable.

Orthodox Judaism greatly limits who is qualified to interpret halachah, and in what way. In the ultra-Orthodox community, only a handful of venerable experts offer *halachic* opinions. Even then, a particular individual or ruling may not be acceptable to all. In the modern Orthodox community, the number of individuals rendering *halachic* judgments is greater, though still restricted to rabbis with advanced training.

THE TEXT

Eliezer Berkovits is a leading Orthodox theologian. He has served as chairman of the Jewish Philosophy Department of the Hebrew Theological College, and he is the author of a number of volumes addressing issues of modern Jewish thought. This text is from The Condition of Jewish Belief, *a symposium compiled by the editors of* Commentary *magazine in 1966.*

But if this is the case, would not any commandment of God, because it expresses His will, have the same religious significance or effect? The answer to this old theological question is Yes: no matter what the contents of the commandments were, man would still be obligated to submit to the will of God and obey them. But it so happened that God revealed and commanded this Torah and not another one, because of His concern for man. As to the meaning of the commandments, even those that apparently have neither ethical nor doctrinal content, one must—as always—refer to the oral tradition, as well as to the continually developing philosophy and theology of Judaism. One may explain the ritual commandments according to Saddia's hedonism, or according to Yehuda Halevi's quasi-mysticism; according to Maimonides's rationalism, or Kabbalistic mysticism, or according to some more sophisticated modern religious philosophy or theology. The commandments, however, remain unchangeably binding.

Probing the Text

1. From an Orthodox perspective, are all the commandments of equal significance?

2. Does reason have a role in revelation or in the observance of *halachah*?

3. How does one decide a *halachic* question on a matter of new technology where there is apparently no precedent?

4. Does Orthodox Judaism reflect a fundamentalist approach to Torah and *halachah*?

A Reform Perspective

APPROACHING THE TEXT
Pittsburgh Platform
San Francisco Platform

The premise of Reform Judaism, that Torah is a humanly written document, has profound implications regarding its view of *halachah*. Orthodox Judaism recognizes the supreme authority of *halachah* because it is God's revealed will. Reform makes no such argument and so has viewed *halachah* differently in various periods of its history.

The Pittsburgh Platform makes a distinction between two kinds of commandments, ethical and ritual. Ethical commandments are generally those involving actions between people. Ritual commandments are usually those involving actions between the individual and God. Of course, there are certain commandments, such as observing the Sabbath, that touch upon both realms. The Pittsburgh Platform looked upon the ethical commandments of the Torah as binding and upon the ritual commandments as conditional on the times. Since ritual commandments had to pass the test of relevance, it is no surprise that early Reform judged many Jewish customs dating from the biblical and rabbinic eras as no longer meaningful. In particular, it scorned rules of attire (such as *kippot* and *tallit*), diet (*kashrut)*, and personal status (priestly regulations, purity, *ketubah*, *get*, etc.).

A marked softening of early Reform's negative attitude toward ritual can be detected in the Columbus and San Francisco Platforms. While the significance of ethics is not diminished, the importance of ritual life is elevated. It is fair to say that the Columbus and San Francisco Platforms recognize that ritual, so long as it evolves, remains central to Judaism.

Even though Reform came to appreciate the place of ritual observance, it maintains a number of crucial distinctions in the observance of *halachah*. Most important, the individual Jew at home, and each community of Jews in their congregation, are free to shape their own pattern of observance. Reform contends that as a humanly created system of law, *halachah* is not infallible. Through study, the wisdom of the collective tradition can be appreciated, but it must be weighed against other considerations including issues of individual conscience, insights from other ethical traditions, and exigencies of time and place. This process of informed decision making is as true for the individual as it is for the congregation. Reform thus maintains that *halachah* can, and should, evolve.

Reform's support of individual autonomy in ritual decisions has been rather severely criticized by traditional Jews on two grounds. The first is that such individual liberty is contrary to the Torah, which obligates all Jews to follow its law. The second objection is that offering freedom to each individual to do as he or she sees fit leads to religious anarchy. Opponents of Reform argue that this kind of anarchy seriously divides the Jewish people and leads to significant assimilation. Proponents of Reform, on the other hand, praise its recognition of individual autonomy as the only true democratic approach to Judaism in the modern age. They generally see the ideological divisions within Judaism as constant and inevitable, and they view Reform not as encouraging, but as preventing, assimilation.

THE TEXT

The three "Platforms of Reform Judaism" are the products of rabbinic gatherings of the movement in 1875 (Pittsburgh), 1937 (Columbus), and 1976 (San Francisco). While not official expressions of doctrine, they have been influential in determining the nature of Reform ideology and practice. The accompanying text is excerpted from the Pittsburgh and San Francisco Platforms.

Pittsburgh Platform 1875

We recognize in the Mosaic legislation a system of training the Jewish people for its mission during its national life in Palestine, and today we accept as binding only the moral laws and maintain only such ceremonies as elevate and sanctify our lives, but reject all such as are not adapted to the views and habits of modern civilization.

We hold that all such Mosaic and Rabbinical laws as regulate diet, priestly purity and dress originated in ages and under the influence of ideas altogether foreign to our present mental and spiritual state. They fail to impress the modern Jew with a spirit of priestly holiness; their observance in our day is apt rather to obstruct than to further modern spiritual elevation.

San Francisco Platform 1976

Torah results from the relationship between God and the Jewish people. The records of our earliest confrontations are uniquely important to us. Lawgivers and prophets, historians and poets gave us a heritage whose study is a religious imperative and whose practice is our chief means to holiness. Rabbis and teachers, philosophers and mystics, gifted Jews in every age amplified the Torah tradition.

Judaism emphasizes action rather than creed as the primary expression of a religious life, the means by which we strive to achieve universal justice and peace. Reform Judaism shares this emphasis on duty and obligation. Our founders stressed that the Jew's ethical responsibilities, personal and social, are enjoined by God. The past century has taught us that the claims made upon us may begin with our ethical obligations but they extend to many other aspects of Jewish living, including: creating a Jewish home centered on family devotion; life-long study; private prayer and public worship; daily religious observance; keeping the Sabbath and the holy days; celebrating the major events of life; involvement with the synagogue and community; and other activities which promote the survival of the Jewish people and enhance its existence. Within each area of Jewish observance Reform Jews are called upon to confront the claims of Jewish tradition, however differently perceived, and to exercise their individual autonomy, choosing and creating on the basis of commitment and knowledge.

Probing the Text

1. How do Reform Jews go about making their own decision on a point of *halachah*?

2. What factors account for the change in Reform attitudes toward ritual observance between the Pittsburgh Platform of 1875 and the San Francisco Platform of 1976?

3. When deciding which *halachah* to observe, what other factors besides traditional law should be taken into account, and what relative weight in the decision-making process should they occupy?

4. Can you give examples of Reform practice in each of the categories of ritual observance specified in the 1976 Platform?

A Conservative Perspective

Approaching the Text

Emet Ve-Emunah

While Conservative Judaism shares with Reform the conviction that Torah is a humanly written document, the Conservative approach to *halachah* is significantly different. Reform does not accept *halachah* as binding; the ultimate decision concerning ritual observance is left to the individual or congregation. Conservative Judaism, to the contrary, does view *halachah* as binding.

A major difference between the two movements is the way in which *halachah* can be changed or modified. Careful reading of the text will reveal that the Conservative movement restricts the agents of *halachic* change to the rabbis. While the voice of their constituency may be important, the decision-making process remains a rabbinic prerogative. The specific body within the Conservative movement that issues *halachic* opinions is the Committee on Jewish Laws and Standards of the Rabbinical Assembly. Those individuals selected to offer *halachic* judgments may come to opposing verdicts. As in the Talmud, the normative judgment usually follows the majority. While procedures have changed over the years, of late the rule has been that if a position is held by all but two or fewer members, it is binding. If three or more oppose, then the minority position is also considered a legitimate option for the Conservative movement.

The voice of the laity can have an important influence on the deliberations of the Conservative rabbinate. Two important and controversial decisions of recent decades were taken in part due to the groundswell of support that emerged among the general membership. In neither case was acceptance of these decisions unanimous. In the first case, the Law Committee voted to permit travel on the Sabbath for the purpose of attending synagogue services. In the second case, the Law Committee agreed to ordain women as rabbis. This followed a series of earlier decisions, going back to the 1950s, that allowed women to be called to the Torah, to be counted in a minyan, and to serve as witnesses in legal proceedings. In almost every controversial case, dissenting minority opinions (of three or more votes) have been offered and thus remain a Conservative option.

THE TEXT

This text is from Emet Ve-Emunah, *subtitled:* Statement of Principles of Conservative Judaism. *It is the unified statement of the movement, published in 1988. Joining in the platform were all three major bodies of the Conservative movement: the Jewish Theological Seminary, the Rabbinical Assembly, and the United Synagogue of America.*

We in the Conservative community are committed to carrying on the rabbinic tradition of preserving and enhancing Halakhah by making the appropriate changes in it through rabbinic decision. This flows from our conviction that Halakhah is indispensable for each age. As in the past, the nature and number of adjustments of the law will vary with the degree of change in the environment in which Jews live. The rapid technological and social change of our time, as well as new ethical insights and goals, have required new interpretations and applications of Halakhah to keep it vital for our lives; more adjustments will undoubtedly be necessary in the future. These include additions to the received tradition to deal with new circumstances and, in some cases, modifications of the corpus of Halakhah.

While change is both a traditional and a necessary part of Halakhah, we, like our ancestors, are not committed to change for its own sake. Hence, the thrust of the Jewish tradition and the Conservative community is to maintain the law and practices of the past as much as possible, and the burden of proof is on the one who wants to alter them. Halakhah has responded and must continue to respond to changing conditions, sometimes through alteration of the law and sometimes by standing firm against passing fads and skewed values. Moreover, the necessity for change does not justify any particular proposal for revision. Each suggestion cannot be treated mechanically but must rather be judged in its own terms, a process which requires thorough knowledge of both Halakhah and the contemporary scene as well as carefully honed skills of judgment.

PROBING THE TEXT

1. What reasons account for the changes in *halachah* that the Conservative movement feels compelled to make?

2. Why is the right to make such changes restricted to rabbis?

3. By what authority does the Conservative movement feel that it is justified in permitting travel on the Sabbath and ordaining women rabbis?

4. How does the Conservative view of adapting *halachah* to contemporary life differ from that of Reform?

A Reconstructionist Perspective

Approaching the Text

Exploring Judaism: A Reconstructionist Approach

Reconstructionism shares a liberal view of revelation in many ways consistent with Reform. As Alpert and Staub state: "Transnaturalism rejects the belief that the words of Torah come from divine revelation at Sinai or that the mitzvot are each divinely ordained commandments." Torah as a humanly written document is the only logical conclusion of Reconstructionist doctrine. Thus it is to be expected that Reconstructionism agrees with Reform on the nonbinding nature of *halachah* and the concept of individual and congregational autonomy.

In fact, Alpert and Staub use the term "Post-*Halachic* Judaism" to describe the Reconstructionist approach. Reform and Reconstructionism have often been criticized for the anarchy that can result from individual freedom to determine ritual observance. Yet as many liberal Jews see it, this is the inescapable predicament of modern times. In the words of one Kaplan disciple, there can be "no retreat from reason."

At the same time, Reconstructionism has always accorded merit to the preservation of ritual life. Although *halachah* requires voluntary consent and should undergo evolutionary change, Kaplan recognized the importance of ritual in Jewish civilization. He called the commandments *sancta:* the means by which a people invested their lives with symbolic and transcendent meaning. In this context we can understand Milton Steinberg's claim that "presumption is always in favor of the tradition." *Halachah* represents the accumulated cultural wisdom of a people over the ages. Tradition can and should be emended, but for good reason.

Alpert and Staub offer the lighting of the Sabbath candles as an example of the abiding significance of ritual. Not only do the candles symbolize the special nature of the Sabbath, they also express the different meanings Jews have attached to them throughout the ages. Some see the light as an invocation of God's presence. Others look upon the candle lighting as ushering in the added soul, or dimension of spirituality, associated with the Sabbath. Today many point to the way in which observing this ritual brings families together.

Before rejecting the past, Alpert and Staub urge that we ask ourselves a series of questions which are designed to "hear the voices of our ancestors" but at the same time to "hear our own voices." Making informed decisions on matters of religious observance is never easy. All the movements of Judaism that admit autonomous decision making require the individual and community to struggle with tradition and change, with the claims of the past and those of the present.

THE TEXT

Rebecca T. Alpert is Dean of Students at the Reconstructionist Rabbinical College in Philadelphia. Jacob J. Staub is editor of the Reconstructionist magazine and Director of the Department of Medieval Civilization at the Reconstructionist Rabbinical College. Together, they coauthored a popular summary of Reconstructionist thought, Exploring Judaism: A Reconstructionist Approach, *from which this text is excerpted.*

From a transnaturalist viewpoint, God is not an omnipotent commander who rewards and punishes. What then is the rationale for obeying Jewish laws? What does it mean, for example, to address God as the one who commands us to light Shabbat candles? In what sense are we commanded?

The answer to this question is found in our initial definition of what it means to see oneself as part of the Jewish people. We behave as Jews because we value our connections to Jewish people, past and present. Jewish rituals have a sacred history that reflect inherited wisdom as well as group renewal. They should not be discarded casually. Otherwise, each generation could begin anew rather than reconstruct.

We often choose to retain the traditional forms of Jewish practice, even when we no longer mean what our ancestors meant when they spoke those words or performed those actions. We do so because such rituals both enrich us and sustain us–leading to our salvation in terms of our own values. Sanctified by the intentionality of our ancestors, the ritual forms themselves are permeated with a sacred aura that is ideally suited to help us deepen our connections to the divine presence.

Thus, when we light the Shabbat candles, we do more than symbolize the beginning of the day of rest devoted to our ultimate values. The flickering candles themselves possess a power to transform us because of the *kavvanot* (meanings) that past generations attributed to those candles.

Kaplan insisted that we preserve and observe Jewish customs and values as long as they continue to serve as a vehicle towards salvation–the enhancement of the meaning and purposefulness of our existence.

When a particular Jewish value or custom is found wanting in this respect, it is our obligation as Jews to find a means to reconstruct it–to adopt innovative practices or find new meanings in old ones.

That the past has a vote means that we must struggle to hear the voices of our ancestors. What did this custom or that idea mean to them? How did they see the presence of God in it? How can we retain or regain its importance in our own lives? That the past does not have a veto means that we must struggle to hear our own voices as distinct from theirs. What might this custom or that idea mean to us today? As participants in a secular civilization, how can we incorporate our values into our lives as Jews?

Probing the Text

1. What criteria would a Reconstructionist employ to judge the importance and continued relevance of a particular commandment, such as the lighting of Sabbath candles?

2. What is the power, and the limitation, of tradition according to the Reconstructionist view?

3. In what way is the Reconstructionist view of *halachah* different from that of Conservative Judaism?

4. How do Alpert and Staub understand Kaplan's famous dictum that *halachah* "has a vote, not a veto"?

Part IV

ISRAEL

Eretz Yisrael, the land of Israel, has always occupied a prominent position in Jewish religious thought. In the Bible, the land of Israel is promised to the descendants of Abraham. For almost a thousand years a Jewish state persisted in the Land of Israel. Surviving wars and outlasting imperial oppression, the people of Israel kept Jerusalem as their capital and Judaism as their religion. Jews returned to Israel after each exile, and a small community clung to the land from the time of the Roman destruction of the Temple in 70 C.E. to the present. During almost two thousand years of Diaspora existence, Jews remembered Israel in their prayers and literature. A movement to reestablish a Jewish state gained momentum in the late 1800s, largely under the leadership of Theodor Herzl. Vision became reality in 1948 when the modern State of Israel was born.

The creation of the State of Israel in 1948 has posed two great questions for contemporary Judaism. The first concerns the nature of the relationship between Israel and the Diaspora. One might think that support for a Jewish state has always been strong and united. Happily today such support for a sovereign Israel is almost unanimous in the Jewish community. But from the beginning of the political Zionist movement until the Holocaust, significant elements in both the Reform and Orthodox communities did not favor the establishment of a new Jewish state. The reasons for their objections will be examined in the texts that follow. But even today, when all four movements recognize Israel's essential place in their own ideology, the exact nature of Israel's place is still at issue. Should Israel be the sole or primary focus of Jewish life? Should *aliyah* (making one's home in Israel) be encouraged? Should Jews in the Diaspora publicly oppose policies of the Jewish state when they think they are wrong?

The other central question involving Israel is: What role should Judaism play in the life of a modern democratic nation which is at the same time the historic Jewish homeland? In particular, what role should *halachah*, traditional Jewish law, assume in a country where the clear majority of Jews do not classify themselves as traditionally observant? These questions have assumed dramatic importance due to the influence of Orthodox parties on the Israeli political process during the last decades. To this day, any Jewish citizen in Israel wishing to marry or divorce, or any individual wishing to convert, must do so according to Orthodox procedures.

In the 1970s and 1980s, the other three Jewish movements became increasingly vocal about what they perceived as the unfair Orthodox monopoly on these matters. The three liberal movements began to protest Orthodoxy's attempts to thwart their growth by denying them governmental funds and building permits. They vigorously opposed legislation introduced by the Orthodox parties which, to their minds, represented religious coercion. Most notable was the campaign by the liberal movements to prevent an amendment to Israel's Law of Return, in regard to Jewish converts, which would have required evidence of conversion according to *halachah* for purposes of citizenship. While this amendment was not instituted, progress in limiting the power of Orthodoxy in other areas is modest or nonexistent. The issue of religious equality and pluralism in the Jewish state remains controversial.

An Orthodox Perspective

Approaching the Text
The Mizrachi Manifesto

Although the Mizrachi Manifesto dates back to the early nineteenth-century, it remains representative of Orthodox Zionist thinking. Like Reform, part of the Orthodox community initially displayed hostility toward Theodor Herzl and the Zionist enterprise. With the Holocaust and creation of the State of Israel, however, the anti-Zionist school diminished. Today only a few ultra-Orthodox sects remain opposed to the State.

Initial Orthodox opposition grew out of two concerns. The first was the belief that a new Israel should come about by Divine, not mortal, initiative. In other words, when God saw fit to establish a third commonwealth, well and good; in the meantime it was necessary to wait and endure. The second factor was fear of what a non-*halachic* state might bring. Even today many Orthodox Jews are dismayed that Torah enjoys only a limited role in Israel's judicial system.

The Manifesto itself envisions an Israel that will be a "secure fortress for our Torah." Not all Orthodox Jews agree that this goal is realizable. They understand that Israel is home to a majority of Jews who call themselves secular as well as to a significant non-Jewish population. Neither do all Orthodox Jews agree with the Manifesto's contention that full Jewish expression is possible only in Israel. Orthodox Jews living in the Diaspora commonly endorse the justification of Diaspora existence expressed in the three other statements of this chapter.

THE TEXT

Mizrachi is a religious Zionist movement founded in Vilna in 1902. It is guided by the motto: "The land of Israel for the people of Israel according to the Torah of Israel". Mizrachi has remained an important Zionist faction throughout Israel's history. This excerpt, in translation, is from its Manifesto.

In the lands of the Diaspora the soul of our people—our Holy Torah—can no longer be preserved in its full strength, nor can the commandments, which comprise the entire spiritual life of the people, be kept in their original purity.

Against his will each loses his Jewish self in the (non-Jewish) majority, for only in their midst can he fulfill all those secular requirements which the times demand of him. The people have found one remedy for this affliction—to direct their hearts to that one place which has always been the focus of our prayers, that place wherein the oppressed of our people will find their longed-for respite: Zion and Jerusalem. We have always been united by that ancient hope, by the promise which lies at the very roots of our religion, namely, that only out of Zion will the Lord bring redemption to the people of Israel. The emancipation which our German brethren so desired did much to divide us and keep us scattered in the countries of our dispersion. When the limbs are dispersed, the body disintegrates, and when there is no body, the spirit has no place to dwell in this world.

It has therefore been agreed by all those who love the spirit of their people and are faithful to their God's Torah, that the reawakening of the hope of the return to Zion will provide a solid foundation as well as lend a special quality to our people. It will serve as a focus for the ingathering of our spiritual forces and as a secure fortress for our Torah and its sanctity.

Probing the Text

1. What is the problem of Diaspora existence according to the Manifesto?

2. What way will the return to Israel effect spiritual renewal for the Jewish people?

3. What role does religion play in the State of Israel as envisioned by Mizrachi?

4. What aspects of Mizrachi's viewpoint might other Orthodox groups find objectionable?

A Reform Perspective

Approaching the Text
San Francisco Platform

The evolution of thought in the San Francisco Platform is rather remarkable. It reflects the dramatic change that transpired as Reform responded to the sweep of Jewish history in this century. While today many might take Reform support of Zionism and Israel for granted, it was not always the case.

The Pittsburgh Platform of 1875 bluntly stated Reform's initial objection to the idea of a Jewish state:

> We consider ourselves no longer a nation, but a religious community, and therefore expect neither a return to Palestine nor the restoration of any of the laws concerning the Jewish state.

Classical Reform stressed the universalistic, ethical impulse of Judaism. Nationalism had little place in that scheme. Ironically, Reform in Germany allied itself with Orthodox circles to oppose the early Zionist Congress gatherings. In all fairness, it should be added that both in Europe and America some individual rabbis remained staunch Zionists even while their respective organizations publicly opposed Zionist activities.

The Columbus Platform of 1937, on the eve of the Holocaust, already reveals a changed movement:

> In the rehabilitation of Palestine, the land hallowed by memories and hopes, we behold the promise of renewed life for many of our brethren. We affirm the obligation of all Jewry to aid in its upbuilding as a Jewish homeland.

The platform goes on to describe Israel as "homeland" in the sense of physical refuge, but also in the sense of a spiritual and cultural center for the Jewish people. Two prominent Reform rabbis, Stephen S. Wise and Abba Hillel Silver, were leading Zionists of their day. Their role in influencing American opinion in support of the newly emerging Jewish state was crucial.

Reform's latest platform enlarges upon the Columbus declaration in three ways. The San Francisco Platform goes as far as to encourage *aliyah* for those in the Reform community who are so inclined. At the same time, it strongly defends the right of Jews to maintain communities wherever they choose. The platform makes explicit the possibility of experiencing a full Jewish life in the Diaspora. Also noteworthy is the call for unconditional recognition of Reform Judaism in Israel. Even today, Israeli law provides that all Jewish religious matters of personal status are under the jurisdiction of the Orthodox rabbinate in Israel. As a result, marriages, conversions, and related ceremonies officiated by non-Orthodox rabbis are not recognized by the State. Neither, for that matter, are civil ceremonies allowed. The fledgling Reform movement in Israel has attempted to contest this arrangement in court, to almost no avail.

The Text

The three "Platforms of Reform Judaism" are the products of rabbinic gatherings of the movement in 1875 (Pittsburgh), 1937 (Columbus) and 1976 (San Francisco). While not official expressions of doctrine, they have been influential in determining the nature of Reform ideology and practice. The accompanying text is excerpted from the San Francisco Platform.

San Francisco Platform 1976

We are privileged to live in an extraordinary time, one in which a third Jewish commonwealth has been established in our people's ancient homeland. We are bound to that land and to the newly reborn State of Israel by innumerable religious and ethnic ties. We have been enriched by its culture and ennobled by its indomitable spirit. We see it providing unique opportunities for Jewish self-expression. We have both a stake and a responsibility in building the State of Israel, assuring its security and defining its Jewish character. We encourage aliyah for those who wish to find maximum personal fulfillment in the cause of Zion. We demand that Reform Judaism be unconditionally legitimized in the State of Israel.

At the same time that we consider the State of Israel vital to the welfare of Judaism everywhere, we reaffirm the mandate of our tradition to create strong Jewish communities wherever we live. A genuine Jewish life is possible in any land, each community developing its own particular character and determining its Jewish responsibilities. The foundation of Jewish community life is the synagogue. It leads us beyond itself to cooperate with other Jews, to share their concerns, and to assume leadership in communal affairs. We are therefore committed to the full democratization of the Jewish community and to its hallowing in terms of Jewish values.

The State of Israel and the diaspora, in fruitful dialogue, can show how a people transcends nationalism even as it affirms it, thereby setting an example for humanity which remains largely concerned with dangerously parochial goals.

Probing the Text

1. What are the "innumerable religious and ethnic ties" that bind the Jewish people to Israel, as referred to in the platform statement?
2. In what way does this statement distinguish itself from classic Zionism?
3. Why is there a specific call for Reform Judaism to be unconditionally recognized in Israel?
4. Why was early Reform Judaism antagonistic toward Zionism?

A Conservative Approach

Approaching the Text
Emet Ve-Emunah

The section of the Conservative platform entitled "The State of Israel and the Role of Religion" acknowledges the State as homeland and haven. Israel is called "a distinctively Jewish state fostering Jewish religious and cultural values." At the same time, however, it is conceived as fully democratic. In the words of the platform: "We do not view Israel as just another state or political entity; rather we envision it as an exemplar of religious and moral principles, of civil, political and religious rights for all citizens."

The Conservative vision articulates what many consider to be a unique, and certainly a challenging and problematic, aspect of modern Israel. On the one hand, Israel aspires to be a full democracy. On the other hand, Israel is not an officially secular state, like most democratic nations. The United States, for example, is constitutionally required to maintain, in Jefferson's words, a wall of separation between church and state. Difficult questions arise from Israel's predicament. Can Israel be fully democratic and at the same time be a "distinctively Jewish state"? What should the role of religion be in matters of government?

This is the backdrop for a strongly worded appeal in the Conservative platform against religious coercion, discrimination, and intolerance in the State of Israel. As with the Reform movement, the status of liberal Judaism in Israel is of major concern to the Conservative movement. The Conservative movement maintains some 30 congregations in Israel, numbering a few thousand individuals. Conservative rabbis are unable to perform marriages and funerals. Like Reform, Conservative Judaism is regularly denigrated by members of Israel's Orthodox community and denied funds provided to the Orthodox establishment. The Conservative movement has been working to change the status quo, but the statement admits that the balancing of democratic and Jewish goals, including equal treatment not only for liberal Jews but for fully secular Jews and non-Jews, "presents a constant challenge."

The second section of the Conservative platform, entitled "Israel and the Diaspora," affirms the attachment of the Jewish people to the land of Israel throughout its long history. Israel's past and present role in Jewish life is described as central. The presence of the Conservative movement within Israel is proudly stressed, yet a clear justification of Diaspora Jewish life is also presented. The platform describes Jewish religion as "land-centered but never land-bound." It reiterates what it sees as the vital role Diaspora centers have played in Jewish history. It calls for a relationship of mutual support and enrichment. Remember that the Reform, Conservative, and Reconstructionist statements included here are products of American movements. It should come as no surprise that their ideologies support their own continued existence!

THE TEXT

This text is from Emet Ve-Emunah, *subtitled:* Statement of Principles of Conservative Judaism. *It is the unified statement of the movement, published in 1988. Joining in the platform were all three major bodies of the Conservative movement: the Jewish Theological Seminary, the Rabbinical Assembly, and United Synagogue of America.*

We rejoice in the existence of *Medinat Yisrael* (the State of Israel) in *Eretz Yisrael* (the Land of Israel) with its capital of Jerusalem, the Holy City, the City of Peace. We view this phenomenon not just in political or military terms; rather, we consider it to be a miracle, reflecting Divine Providence in human affairs. We glory in that miracle; we celebrate the rebirth of Zion.

We staunchly support the Zionist ideal and take pride in the achievement of the State of Israel in the gathering of our people from the lands of our dispersion and in rebuilding a nation. The State of Israel and its well-being remain a major concern of the Conservative movement, as of all loyal Jews. To be sure, the Conservative movement has not always agreed with Israel's positions on domestic and foreign affairs. We have often suffered from discriminatory policies, but we remain firm and loving supporters of the State of Israel economically, politically, and morally.

We view it as both a misinterpretation of Jewish history and a threat to Jewish survival to negate the complementary roles of *Eretz Yisrael* and the Diaspora. Currently there are various important centers of Jewish life in the Diaspora. Diaspora Jewry furnishes vital economic, political and moral support to Israel; Israel imbues Diaspora Jewry with a sense of pride and self-esteem. Some see the role of *Medinat Yisrael* as the cultural and religious center of world Jewry. Others insist that since the days of the Prophets, various foci or centers of Jewish life and civilization, in both Israel and the Diaspora, have sustained the creative survival of *Am Yisrael* and *Torat Yisrael.*

PROBING THE TEXT

1. How is this statement similar to that of the Reform platform?
2. How do Israel and the Diaspora mutually support each other?
3. What is meant by the term "miracle" in this passage?
4. What "discriminatory policies" by the State of Israel against the Conservative Movement are being alluded to in this statement?

A Reconstructionist Perspective

Approaching the Text
Tradition and Change

Milton Steinberg offers two basic rationales for the direct link he perceives between Zionism and Reconstructionism. Each one appeals to an aspect of Reconstructionism's broad view of Judaism not only as an institutional religion but as a complete civilization. Like Conservative Judaism, but unlike Reform and Orthodox, the Reconstructionist movement was Zionist oriented from its inception and did not have within its ranks a dissenting school.

The first rationale for the Reconstructionist's tie to Zionism is ethnic in nature. Israel is a refuge for Jews around the world. It is the second largest community of Jews in the world; anyone concerned with the welfare of the Jewish people is necessarily supportive of Israel's well-being. Like any other people the Jews have every right to their own homeland and the basic security that derives from such a place.

The second rationale is historical and cultural in nature. Characteristic of Jewish history is the presence of the Jewish people in the land of Israel. Even after Jewish sovereignty was denied and the Jewish people dispersed, the land of Israel and the hope for regained sovereignty remained part of Jewish liturgy, law, and lore. Jewish civilization, as history demonstrates, is not wholly dependent on land but is intimately tied to it. Given the hardships imposed upon the flowering of Jewish culture, even in our day, the imperative for a Jewish homeland remains as strong as ever. As Steinberg puts it: "Somewhere in the world it [Jewish culture] must be the dominant concern of Jews."

Steinberg concludes in a fashion similar to the Reform and Conservative statements by disassociating Reconstructionism from those Zionists who negate the Diaspora. Mordecai Kaplan had argued from the beginning of the movement that Diaspora Jews could flourish Jewishly in America. He noted that doing this would entail shouldering the burden of living in two civilizations: secular American democracy and sectarian Jewish culture. But Kaplan pointed out that this fact of existence could give rise to a creative tension, of the kind that had contributed immensely to Jewish thought and culture throughout the 2,000-year history of the Diaspora. Like Reform and Conservative thinkers, Kaplan claimed that the historical study of Judaism revealed a religion and culture in continuous dynamic interaction with cultures around it. Judaism, according to this theory, survived because it was able to absorb and evolve. The Diaspora, according to Kaplan, should remain a spiritual center, like the reborn Jewish State, for the rejuvenation of Judaism.

The Reconstructionist movement, small even in the United States, does not have an organizational structure in Israel, save for one congregation that has long been sympathetic to the Reconstructionist outlook. Joining with its sister liberal Jewish movements, however, the Reconstructionists have supported close ties with the Jewish State and at the same time protested the inequality among the movements of Judaism in Israel.

THE TEXT

Milton Steinberg (1903–1950) was a congregational rabbi, author, and leading figure in the young Reconstructionist movement. Like others of his generation, he was trained in the Conservative movement and, although profoundly influenced by Kaplan, differed with him at times.

To put the matter bluntly, Reconstructionism leads directly to Zionism. Given the premises of the first, the second follows relentlessly.

1) No program for the perpetuation of Judaism can be indifferent to the welfare of the people who are its bearers. Palestine has saved the lives of myriad Jews in the past, it promises to redeem many more in the future. On this score, alone, Reconstructionism must indorse Zionism.

2) There is in Reconstructionism a heavy bias in favor of the historical in Judaism. The love of Zion, the hope of its rebuilding, the dream of the restoration there of at least a part of the Jewish people are etched deep and indelible in the consciousness of the Jewish traditionalist. In effect, it is next to impossible to accept the Jewish civilization without embracing Zionism at the same time.

3) The Jews constitute, as we have seen, not only a religious communion and a culture group but a people also. And every people ought to have some place in the world where its peoplehood can find total expression.

4) Reconstructionism implies Zionism because of the needs of Judaism, because of the persistent disadvantages we have just surveyed under which Jewish culture operates everywhere. The second civilization of Jews, Judaism is constantly under the necessity of refreshing itself from a free-flowing source. Somewhere in the world it must be the dominant concern of Jews. In other words, a Jewish Homeland must be established.

By the same token, Reconstructionism offers no sympathy or asylum to the Zionism that sees only Palestinian Jewry and no other. There is a Zionist who is so thoroughly absorbed in his distant task that he forgets his Jewish obligations nearer to home. There is another Zionist who despairs of the possibility of Jewish life outside Palestine. Convinced that Diaspora Judaism is doomed, he concentrates his energies on the only Jewry that appears to him to have a chance. With such pessimism, Reconstructionism has no patience. It has confidence in the future of Judaism throughout the world. It objects to the notion that Palestine and the Diaspora are competitive and mutually exclusive. It holds such an alternative to be false and to obscure the job of modern Jews which is not a matter of "either ... or" but of "both."

PROBING THE TEXT

1. According to Steinberg, why is Reconstructionism inherently Zionist?

2. Which of the reasons—ethnic, historical, or cultural—do you find most compelling?

3. What concerns does this statement share with the Reform and Conservative positions already examined?

4. What does it mean to describe Israel as a cultural or spiritual center?

Conclusion

Our study of the sources in this book lead to some broad conclusions. Before stating them, however, it is worthwhile to remember the following caveats:

- not everyone will agree that these texts accurately represent their movement.
- no one text may be able to represent an entire movement.
- individuals within one branch of Judaism may hold widely divergent viewpoints.
- all sources can be interpreted in different ways.
- all conclusions tend toward oversimplification, and are open to dispute.

Keeping in mind all these cautions, my own conclusions are as follows:

God

On the issue of God, the Jewish ideological spectrum is framed by two basic positions:

The first can be termed (rather awkwardly) "theosupernaturalism," belief in a God who is above nature and who creates and rules the world.

The second conception can be called (also clumsily) "theotransnaturalism," belief in a God who works through nature and who is not considered to be infinitely powerful.

Orthodox Judaism adheres to the former position. Reconstructionist Judaism clearly espouses the latter. Reform and Conservative Judaism generally abstain from officially siding with either view; their members include adherents of both schools.

Torah

On the issue of Torah, the Jewish ideological spectrum is also framed by two basic positions:

The first view holds that the Torah is God-given and restricted to the revelation at Sinai.

The second view holds that the Torah is humanly written and part of an ongoing process of revelation or discovery.

Orthodox Judaism champions the former idea. Conservative, Reform, and Reconstructionist Judaism uphold the latter notion of Torah. Remember, however, that the conclusions the movements draw from their shared liberal view of revelation vary.

HALACHAH

On the issue of *halachah*, the Jewish ideological spectrum is framed by three basic positions:

The first posits the absolute authority of *halachah*, which is subject to no change and limited rabbinic interpretation.

The second position upholds the continuing authority of *halachah*, which is subject to cautious change and broader rabbinic interpretation.

The third position supports the conditional authority of *halachah*, which is subject to considerable change and the autonomous decision making of individual Jews.

Orthodox Judaism identifies with the first position. Conservative Judaism has staked out a position reflected by the second view. Reform and Reconstructionist Judaism advocate the third position.

ISRAEL

On the issue of Zionism and Israel, the Jewish ideological spectrum is framed by a unanimity of opinion. This unanimity does not mean that the various branches accept the classical Zionist position that Israel is the only legitimate place for the Jewish people. It does mean, however, that the branches of contemporary American Judaism view Israel as a Jewish homeland and a spiritual center. Of course, no unanimity of opinion exists concerning the extent to which Israel should be governed by civil law or *halachah*.

This book has been written because I believe it is important to recognize our differences in belief, in order to understand and tolerate our diversity of opinion and action. Yet it is also important to recognize our common ground, in order to appreciate what binds us together as a people.

Having explored and learned, it is now time to determine what you believe, and what you will do.

List of Sources

1. Samson Raphael Hirsch, *The Nineteen Letters of Ben Uzziel*. New York: Feldheim, 1969, p. 31. Reprinted by permission.

2. *An Overview Of Reform Judaism*. New York: Union of American Hebrew Congregations, 1983, pp. 16, 24. The platforms were originally published in various editions of the Central Conference of American Rabbis Yearbook. Reprinted by permission.

3. *Emet Ve-Emunah: Statement of Principles of Conservative Judaism*. New York: Rabbinical Assembly (with the Jewish Theological Seminary and United Synagogue of America), 1988, p.18. Reprinted by permission.

4. Mordecai Kaplan, *The Meaning Of God In Modern Jewish Religion*. New York: Reconstructionist Press, 1962 (1937), p. 89. Reprinted by permission.

5. Norman Lamm, in *The Condition of Jewish Belief*. New York: Macmillan Publishing Co., 1967, p. 124. Reprinted by permission.

6. Julian Morgenstern, in *The Growth of Reform Judaism*. New York: World Union for Progressive Judaism, 1965, p. 231. Reprinted by permission.

7. *Emet Ve-Emunah*, pp. 19—20.

8. *Reconstructionist Prayer Book* as quoted in *Tradition and Change*. New York: Rabbinical Assembly, 1958, p. 346. Reprinted by permission.

9. Eliezer Berkovits, in *The Condition of Jewish Belief*, p. 25.

10. *An Overview of Reform Judaism*, pp. 11, 12, 16, 17, 19, 24, 25.

11. *Emet Ve-Emunah*, pp. 23, 24.

12. Rebecca T. Alpert and Jacob J. Staub, *Exploring Judaism: A Reconstructionist Approach.* New York: Reconstructionist Press, 1985, pp. 23, 31. Reprinted by permission.

13. The Mizrachi Manifesto, in *The Jew in the Modern World.* New York: Oxford University Press, 1980, p. 436. Reprinted by permission.

14. *An Overview of Reform Judaism*, pp. 25, 26.

15. *Emet Ve-Emunah*, pp. 37–39.

16. Milton Steinberg, in *Tradition and Change.* pp. 259-260.